Extreme SPORTS No Limits!

Extreme Sports

John Crossingham & Bobbie Kalman

Crabtree Publishing Company

www.crabtreebooks.com

Created by Bobbie Kalman

Dedicated by Amanda Bishop
For the team

Editor-in-Chief
Bobbie Kalman

Writing team
John Crossingham
Bobbie Kalman

Substantive editor
Amanda Bishop

Project editor
Kelley MacAulay

Editors
Molly Aloian
Rebecca Sjonger
Kathryn Smithyman

Art director
Robert MacGregor

Design
Katherine Berti

Production coordinator
Heather Fitzpatrick

Photo research
Crystal Sikkens

Consultants
Kerry Graeber, Vice President and Director of Communications,
    AMA Pro Racing
Scott Starr, Skateboarding/Snowboarding Photographer/Historian
Paul West, President, United States Surfing Federation

Special thanks to
Burton Snowboards, MBS Mountainboards

Photographs
AP/Wide World Photos: pages 8, 11 (left), 26 (bottom)
Patrick Batchelder: page 27 (middle)
Burton Snowboards: page 5
© Royalty-Free/CORBIS: pages 19 (top), 23 (right)
Digital Vision: pages 4, 21, 25 (bottom)
© Tony Donaldson/Icon SMI: page 26 (top)
www.kevinkleinphotography.com: page 14
© Andrew Malana/Icon SMI: page 27 (top)
PhotoDisc: pages 19 (bottom), 25 (top and middle), 28
Shazamm: pages 9, 10, 13 (right),
MBS Mountainboards: Steve Bonini: page 15
© STL/Icon SMI: page 27 (bottom)
Other images by Adobe Image Library, Corbis Images, and PhotoDisc

Crabtree Publishing Company

www.crabtreebooks.com1-800-387-7650

Copyright © **2004 CRABTREE PUBLISHING COMPANY.**All
rights reserved. No part of this publication may be reproduced, stored in a
retrieval system or be transmitted in any form or by any means, electronic,
mechanical, photocopying, recording, or otherwise, without the prior
written permission of Crabtree Publishing Company. In Canada: We
acknowledge the financial support of the Government of Canada through
the Canada Book Fund for our publishing activities.

Printed in the U.S.A./112013/CG20130917

Library of Congress Cataloging-in-Publication Data
Crossingham, John.
  Extreme sports / John Crossingham & Bobbie Kalman.
    v. cm. -- (Extreme sports no limits series)
  Includes index.
  Contents: Going to the extreme--Humble beginnings--X marks the sport--
Hitting the road--The wheels turn--On top of the world--Chill! --On board--
Water and wind--Making waves--What goes up must come down--Extreme
closeups--Playing safe.
    ISBN 0-7787-1673-2 (RLB) -- ISBN 0-7787-1719-4 (pbk.)
  1. Extreme sports--Juvenile literature. [1. Extreme sports. 2. Sports.] I. Kalman,
Bobbie. II. Title. III. Extreme sports no limits!
  GV749.7.C76 2004
  796.04'6--dc22
                                                          2003027695
                                                          LC

Published in Canada
Crabtree Publishing
616 Welland Ave.
St. Catharines, Ontario
L2M 5V6

Published in the United States
Crabtree Publishing
PMB 59051
350 Fifth Avenue, 59th Floor
New York, New York 10118

Published in the United Kingdom
Crabtree Publishing
Maritime House
Basin Road North, Hove
BN41 1WR

Published in Australia
Crabtree Publishing
3 Charles Street
Coburg North
VIC, 3058

CONTENTS

GOING TO THE EXTREME

Extreme sports are some of today's hottest sports. They are described as "extreme" because they often involve high risks and loads of creativity. Some of these sports are dangerous and some are strange, but all of them are exciting—for athletes and spectators!

ON THE EDGE

Many extreme sports are **individual sports**, which means the athletes perform alone. Competitors in sports such as **BMX biking**, however, may travel as part of a **team**. Extreme sports test the limits of athletes' abilities. Some athletes even risk their lives to improve their skills. This doesn't mean that all extreme sports are dangerous, however. Some sports are simply unusual. Most extreme athletes enjoy being different from other athletes. It's part of what makes them—and their sports—unique.

SPEAKING THE LANGUAGE

Extreme athletes have their own terms to describe moves, equipment, and styles. Some of these terms relate to only one sport, but a few words are used in several sports. For example, many sports have a **freestyle**, or a style that allows the athletes to be as creative as possible. Specific **tricks**, or moves, are regularly given unusual names by their creators. Names and terms are all part of the extreme sports **culture**. A culture is a set of values shared by a group of people. Culture also includes music, clothing, and magazines that athletes and their fans enjoy.

A BRAND NEW WORLD

This book describes extreme sports that are done on land, in water, on mountainsides, and even in midair! Some are popular all over the world, whereas others are so new that many people have never even heard of them.

EXTREME DANGER

This book is full of thrilling photos, but these athletes are experts. They are very experienced and have been practicing their amazing skills and dangerous moves for years. Do not try anything shown in this book!

OFF TO A SLOW START

The term "extreme sports" is new, but many of the events are old—some are even ancient! For example, 4,000 years ago the Native peoples of the Far North used small boats called **kayaks** to hunt walruses, fish, and even small whales. Kayaks were not used for fun—northern peoples needed them to survive. Today, **kayaking** (see page 23) is a popular extreme sport.

Surfing, or riding waves on wooden boards, began over a thousand years ago on the Polynesian islands in the South Pacific Ocean. Slowly, the sport spread to the islands of Hawaii as well. Hawaiian surfers started visiting the United States in the early 1900s, and the athletes' smooth, strong skills amazed Americans. Soon, the whole country wanted to surf!

CATCHING ON

Surfing isn't the only extreme sport that took a long time to catch on. The sport of **rock climbing** slowly developed as mountain climbers began traveling up steeper slopes. Teens were diving off cliffs in Mexico as early as the 1930s, but it wasn't until the 1950s that people in the United States first saw films of **cliff diving**. In the 1950s, **motocross**, or motorcycle racing, was popular only in Europe. When the best European motocross bikers traveled to the United States, the sport caught on quickly.

SIDEWALK SURFING U.S.A.

Skateboarding (see page 10) was the first extreme sport to be invented in the United States. In the late 1950s, surfing was a popular sport, but many people did not live near water. The first skateboards were made so people could "surf" on the streets. Some of the first boards were even called "sidewalk surfers." Skateboarders struggled for the next 40 years to gain recognition and respect. Today, "skating" is one of the most popular extreme sports in the world.

X MARKS THE SPORT

Between the 1960s and 1980s, extreme sports were not popular. In fact, many people spoke out against them. They believed that the music and fashions that were favored by surfers and skaters led to disruptive behavior. Many communities tried to ban the sports, and they sometimes succeeded. Extreme athletes didn't give up, though.

They continued to practice their sports in small numbers, forming teams with fellow athletes. Some even started magazines that featured new equipment and top performers. People also began making movies about the stars, the experts, and the hot spots of extreme sports. Magazines, clubs, and films reached all kinds of new fans.

It's crazy, but I like it!

By the late 1980s, extreme sports were gaining popularity. The sports gave people a chance to try something daring. Skateboarding grew so popular that people on BMX bikes, snowboards, and in-line skates started imitating and adapting their favorite skateboarding tricks. People began to use the term "extreme sports" and developed a new respect for extreme athletes.

Let the games begin

In 1995, ESPN hosted the first **X Games**. Athletes from around the world competed to win medals in extreme events while the world watched them on TV. The X Games and **Gravity Games**, which started in 1999, gave extreme athletes a place to showcase their talents. Extreme events such as snowboarding and kayaking have even become part of the Olympic Games!

HITTING THE ROAD

Extreme road sports are among the most popular extreme sports today. Many of them can be done just about anywhere, from skateparks to driveways. Road sports such as skateboarding and **aggressive in-line skating** allow athletes to learn at their own pace and to come up with creative new ways of using their equipment.

Type: individual
Surface: streets, ramps
Born: 1950s

SKATEBOARDING

Skateboarders perform exciting tricks that require steady balance and smooth movements. There are two main styles of skateboarding—**vertical** or "vert" and **street**. Vert skaters ride large ramps called **halfpipes** and perform tricks in the air known as **aerials**. Street skaters prefer to ride **obstacles**, or objects, such as curbs and stair railings, which are everywhere. Favorite tricks include **flips**, **grabs**, and **grinds**.

Type: individual
Surface: streets
Born: late 1970s

Type: individual
Surface: streets, ramps
Born: 1980s

STREET LUGE

The sport of **street luge** started when kids tried racing down hills by lying on skateboards. Today's **luges** are a combination of skateboards and the metal luges used at the Winter Olympics. Street lugers steer their luges by leaning their bodies in the direction of the turn. Lugers wear helmets, gloves, and tough bodysuits called **leathers** for protection. Since street luges don't have brakes, racers also wear thick-soled shoes. They drag their feet along the ground to stop.

AGGRESSIVE IN-LINE SKATING

Aggressive in-line skating, also known as "aggro," started after in-line skaters tried to perform their own versions of skateboarding tricks. Like skateboarding, aggro also has vert and street styles and the same obstacles, such as railings and ramps. Since the wheels are attached to the feet of in-line skaters, these athletes can perform incredible flips and **spins**, or turns in midair, that are impossible to perform on skateboards.

11

THE WHEELS TURN

Motocross, BMX, and **snocross** races are high-speed sports that thrill spectators. Not to be outdone by other freestylers, however, these athletes also use their racing machines for gravity-defying aerials. Riders use ramps or mounds of dirt or snow as launches for incredible airborne shows.

MOTOCROSS

The off-road motorcycle racing called motocross dates back to the 1920s, when it was called **scrambles**. Today, motocross is a sport with many styles and variations. Motocross or "MX" features short races on looped dirt courses that are full of bumps, bends, and sloped curves called **berms**. **Supercross** is an MX race held inside a stadium on a dirt course built using bulldozers. In freestyle MX, riders do not race one another. Instead, the bikers perform daring aerial moves that are similar to grab tricks in skateboarding.

Type: *individual, team*
Surface: *dirt, grass, mud, ramps*
Born: *1920s*

Dirt bikes are lighter and less powerful than street motorcycles. Their weaker engines make them easier to control on tricky MX courses.

BMX

BMX stands for "bicycle motocross." The bikes are specially designed for races that are just like MX races. Instead of motors, however, BMX riders use pure leg power! While racing, BMX riders began performing fancy aerial moves off jumps on courses. Soon, they were using large dirt ramps strictly for jumping and doing tricks. When BMXers tried cycling on the obstacles in skateparks, they found that they were able to perform flips and spins as exciting as any skateboarding tricks.

Type: individual, team
Surface: dirt, grass, mud, ramps
Born: 1970s

SNOCROSS

Winter weather may ruin an MX race, but cold weather is perfect for snocross! Instead of dirt bikes, racers use snowmobiles to tackle icy bumps and snowy berms. Some snocross courses have loops similar to those on MX courses. Other races are huge cross-country events that last for hours! In **hillcross** races, snowmobilers race downhill. Freestyle snocross athletes perform aerial tricks in the same way that motocross and BMX freestyle riders do.

Type: individual, team
Surface: snow
Born: 1980s

ON TOP OF THE WORLD

Some extreme sports take place on extreme landscapes. People all over the world go up into the mountains to test their skills. **Mountain biking** and **mountain boarding** are two of the many sports done on rocky slopes.

MOUNTAIN BIKING

Mountain biking or "MTB" has been popular since the 1980s. Cyclists race on dirt paths, between trees, through mud, and down steep, rocky slopes. Mountain bikes are built to be ridden almost anywhere. Their strong wheels have wide, grooved tires to grip uneven surfaces. Mountain bike races can be as short as a few minutes, but some of the longest last 24 hours. That means the cyclists race one another all day and all night without any rest! These incredible races test the **endurance** of bikers. Endurance is the ability to cycle over long distances and for long periods of time.

Type: individual, team
Surface: hills, rocks, dirt
Born: 1970s

MOUNTAIN BOARDING

Mountain boarding originated as a way to ride skateboards on rough **terrain**, or areas of land. The boards are longer than average skateboards and have four big, inflatable tires. Devices called **shocks** provide a spring to cushion the ride. Mountain boarders strap their feet to their boards so they will not lose control during tricks.

A BUMPY RIDE

Mountain boarders perform tricks that are similar to skateboarding moves. Instead of wooden ramps or long stair railings, however, these athletes jump off rocky ledges or down steep hillsides. Mountain boarders also compete in **slalom** races in which boarders weave around flags called **gates**.

Type: individual
Surface: hills, rocks, dirt
Born: 1970s

CHILL!

Sometimes extreme locations aren't enough to challenge athletes. Some **professionals** or "pros" also want to perform in extreme weather! Extreme snow sports take place in cold, unpredictable weather, making them more difficult. The open spaces of the North allow pros to test their creativity and to experiment with new tricks. These landscapes provide a lot of room for athletes to practice their sports.

Type: individual
Surface: snow
Born: 1980s

FREESKIING

Downhill skiing has been around for over a hundred years, but **freeskiing** has broken new ground for the sport. Freeskiers tackle areas where few winter athletes dare to go, such as rocky cliffs or steep, forested hills. These skiers even use helicopters to fly to locations that are difficult to reach on foot.

Skiing in areas reached only by helicopters is called **heliskiing**. Some freeskiers also like to add the extra challenge of racing one another down a mountain. At such high speeds, freeskiers must have excellent control to avoid nasty collisions with trees and rocks. A **wipeout**, or fall, can be deadly on such steep slopes.

SNOWBOARDING

Snowboarding combines the extreme speed of skiing, the radical tricks of skateboarding, and the smooth moves of surfing. There are three main styles of snowboarding—freestyle, slalom alpine racing, and **freeride**. Freestylers perform aerial stunts such as spins, flips, and grabs. For competitions, a wide ditch made of snow acts as a halfpipe. Competitors move from side to side in the ditch while performing tricks. **Big-air** freestyle competitors launch themselves off huge snow-covered ramps to perform amazing aerial tricks. Alpine racers weave expertly between gates in timed competitions. Freeride snowboarding (shown below) is not about competing. Instead, the snowboarders hike up mountains to ride on **powder**, or newly fallen snow.

Type: individual
Surface: snow
Born: 1980s

17

ON BOARD

Type: individual
Surface: water
Born: over 1,000 years ago

A thousand years ago, surfing tested the courage of those who dared to face powerful waves. Today, surfing is a favorite activity around the world, inspiring all kinds of **variations**, or different types of surfing. With nothing but a board separating the athletes from the waves and sand, all types of surfing are spectacular to watch.

SURFING

Surfers need balance and strength to ride crashing waves! They use two main types of surfboards. **Shortboards** are used to perform sharp turns and flashy tricks. A shortboard is perfect for powerful waves. **Longboards** are more difficult to turn but are great for cruising smaller waves. Beginners usually ride longboards because these boards are very stable. Pro surfers perform balancing tricks on longboards. One such trick is **hanging ten**, or placing all ten toes over the front end of a board. Dedicated surfers travel the world searching for the ultimate waves.

BODYBOARDING

Bodyboarding is like surfing while lying down. A bodyboard is only about 40 inches (101 cm) long. Riders usually lie flat on their boards as waves launch them up to 15 feet (4.6 m) into the air! A bodyboard can be **maneuvered**, or controlled, because the board is held so close to the body. Riders choose their boards based on what they want to do while they ride. Designers are always creating new boards that offer better speed and the ability to perform slick turns.

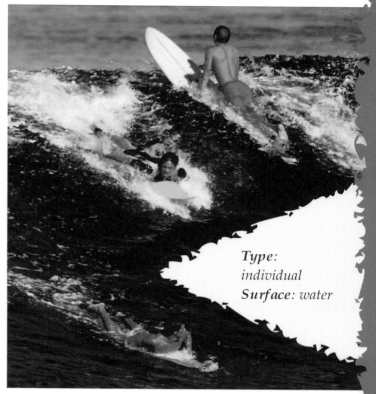

Type: individual
Surface: water

Type: individual
Surface: sand
Born: 1960s

SANDBOARDING

Sandboarding athletes perform elegant turns as they speed down **dunes**, or sand hills. Early sandboarders rode almost anything they could find, even water skis. When snowboarding took off in the 1980s, sandboarders borrowed design ideas from snowboarding to improve their boards. Sandboards are nearly identical to snowboards, but they use a different **wax**, or coating, on the bottom of the board. This wax allows the board to slide smoothly over sand.

WATER AND WIND

Extreme athletes often battle the forces of nature. **Windsurfing** and **kitesurfing** pros take on two of these forces at once—water and wind. These athletes ride the waves while trying to harness the power of moving air. Their colorful equipment seems dull compared to their incredible skills!

WINDSURFING

Few lakes and rivers have waves that can be used for surfing, but windsurfing allows people to "surf" these waters by attaching a sail to a surfboard. A windsurfer holds on to the sail by grabbing an oval bar called a **wishbone**. Holding a wishbone requires great arm strength, especially in high winds. Extreme windsurfers ride their boards on large surfing waves. They are able to jump off the waves and perform wild spins and twists.

Type: individual
Surface: water
Born: 1960s

*Windsurfers often seek out spots with extreme wind called **wind tunnels**. A wind tunnel gives extreme windsurfers excellent speed and great waves for jumps and tricks.*

Kitesurfing

Kitesurfing is similar to windsurfing, but it also resembles **waterskiing**. The surfer holds on to a "kite" that looks like a wide parachute. The kite uses the wind's power to drag the surfer across the water.

The kites are so high that kitesurfers can even hang from them and perform leaps and spins as they jump above waves. Kitesurfboards are much shorter than most surfboards. Their small size is ideal for doing spins and turns.

Type: *individual*
Surface: *water*
Born: *1990s*

Kitesurfers compete in endurance races to see how far they can surf. Some endurance races are held in stages over a couple of days.

MAKING WAVES

Type: individual
Surface: water
Born: 1980s

Extreme athletes find all kinds of ways to conquer waves. Some, such as **wakeboarding** pros, combine elements of different water and land sports. **Barefoot jumping** athletes imitate different sports, too—but without using any equipment! Still others, such as kayaking pros, take on the power of raging waters in tiny boats.

WAKEBOARDING

Wakeboarding is an extreme style of waterskiing that features tricks similar to street skateboarding tricks. Instead of two skis, a wakeboarder uses a small board that looks like a kitesurfboard. Wakeboarders are towed over the water at high speeds behind a powerboat. They use the **wake**, or waves created by the boat moving through water, as ramps to launch themselves into the air. Once airborne, wakeboarders perform spins, flips, and grab tricks. Each series of tricks is called a **routine**.

Type: individual
Surface: water
Born: about 4,000 years ago

Type: individual
Surface: water
Born: 1990s

KAYAKING

Kayaking is done by steering a narrow boat with a double-ended paddle. A kayaker sits in the boat and is completely covered from the waist down by the boat's **shell**, or body. The most daring kayaking occurs in crashing rivers or on strong seas. These areas are called **white water** because the water has plenty of white **crests**, or peaks. White-water kayakers must paddle against strong **currents**, or moving water, to avoid sharp rocks and other hazards. There are many styles of kayaking, including freestyle and several types of racing.

BAREFOOT JUMPING

Barefoot jumping combines the feeling of walking on water with the thrill of flying through the air. Jumpers take off from large ramps and land with great balance. The jumpers are towed behind boats at over 40 miles per hour (64 kph). They then use fiberglass ramps to jump about 15 feet (4.5 m) above the water. Once in the air, they perform tricks or try to jump as far as possible. Jumpers often wear helmets, face guards, and padded suits. During a wipeout, the water's surface can feel as hard as concrete!

WHAT GOES UP, MUST COME DOWN

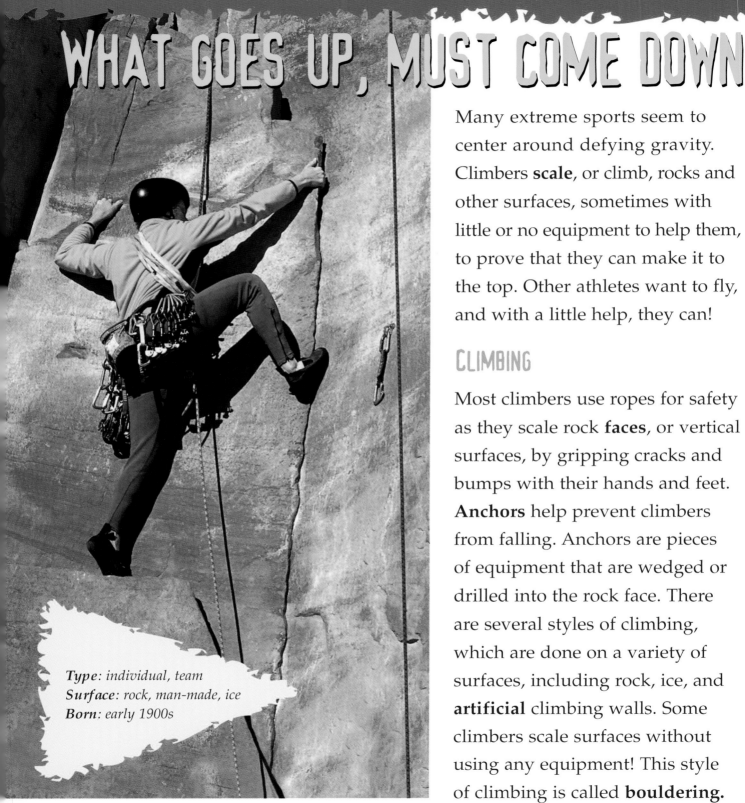

Many extreme sports seem to center around defying gravity. Climbers **scale**, or climb, rocks and other surfaces, sometimes with little or no equipment to help them, to prove that they can make it to the top. Other athletes want to fly, and with a little help, they can!

CLIMBING

Most climbers use ropes for safety as they scale rock **faces**, or vertical surfaces, by gripping cracks and bumps with their hands and feet. **Anchors** help prevent climbers from falling. Anchors are pieces of equipment that are wedged or drilled into the rock face. There are several styles of climbing, which are done on a variety of surfaces, including rock, ice, and **artificial** climbing walls. Some climbers scale surfaces without using any equipment! This style of climbing is called **bouldering.**

Type: *individual, team*
Surface: *rock, man-made, ice*
Born: *early 1900s*

SKYDIVING AND SKYSURFING

Skydiving (top) is the act of **freefalling**, or jumping out of a plane through the open air, with a parachute to slow the fall. Some divers also **skysurf**, or jump with a board attached to their feet and ride the air, just as surfers ride waves. Skysurfers perform dizzying spins and grab tricks with their boards.

Type: individual, team
Surface: air
Born: (surfers) 1980s, (skydivers) 1950s

PARAGLIDING

Paragliding (middle) is done when a person flies across the sky by using wide, inflatable wings. A good paraglider can fly for hours and climb over 10,000 feet (3,048 m) in the air. Paragliders take off by running down gentle hillsides with their wings already open. As they run, the wings lift off the ground, and the gliding begins!

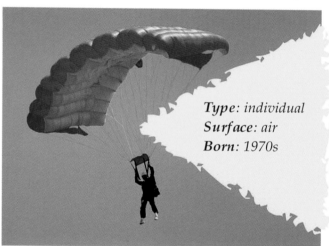

Type: individual
Surface: air
Born: 1970s

CLIFF DIVING

Cliff diving (bottom) involves leaping off mountainsides that are over 100 feet (30.5 m) above water. Athletes enter the water at speeds of 55 miles per hour (88 kph)! Divers can injure themselves unless they hold their bodies straight and pointed down toward the water. Before diving, divers must check the depth of the water and watch for rocky obstacles on the sea floor.

Type: individual
Surface: water
Born: 1930s

EXTREME CLOSEUPS

Some of the biggest names in sports today are those of extreme athletes. These pioneers and stars can be seen everywhere, from TV to magazines to video games. Most are pros—they get paid to be exceptional athletes. The pros on these pages have all broken new ground in their sports!

SKATEBOARDING: TONY HAWK

American skateboarding legend Tony Hawk was amazing people with his skills in vert skating before he was even a teenager. His incredible ability has drawn a huge following, increasing skating's popularity every year for the past twenty years. He has won countless medals in competitions and is still one of the sport's top contenders.

BMX: DAVE MIRRA

American rider Dave Mirra, also known as "Miracle Boy," has been riding since he was only four years old. He was a pro by the time he finished high school! He is a leader in BMX freestyle and holds more X Games gold medals in BMX than does any other competitor.

AGGRESSIVE IN-LINE: FABIOLA DA SILVA

Brazilian Fabiola Da Silva is among the top vert and street in-line skaters competing today. She also holds more X Games medals than any other female competitor in any event. She has consistently won gold or silver medals since 1996—and she started competing only in 1995!

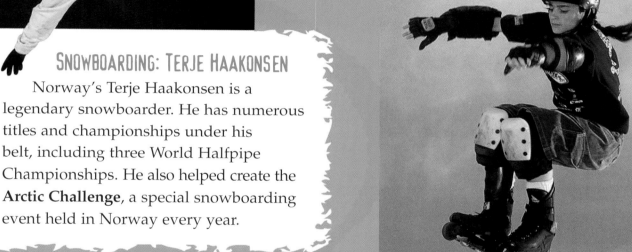

SNOWBOARDING: TERJE HAAKONSEN

Norway's Terje Haakonsen is a legendary snowboarder. He has numerous titles and championships under his belt, including three World Halfpipe Championships. He also helped create the **Arctic Challenge**, a special snowboarding event held in Norway every year.

SURFING: LAYNE BEACHLEY

Australian Layne Beachley is one of the world's best surfers. She has won the women's world title no fewer than five times! She also devotes much of her time to promoting her sport and working as a commentator at surfing events.

PLAYING SAFEL

Extreme athletes have hazardous jobs—their sports are often very dangerous. An injury can keep an athlete out of the game for days, weeks, or even for good. In order to prevent injuries, athletes must always play it safe. Each sport has its own safety precautions. Some of the most common—and most important—are safety gear and equipment maintenance.

IN GEAR

Specific safety gear varies from sport to sport, but most extreme athletes, such as the skydivers shown left, wear helmets to protect their heads. Helmets come in different styles, shapes, and sizes, so there are many options when it comes to picking the most appropriate one. Other safety gear protects the chest, backbone, and joints such as the knees, elbows, and wrists. Proper footwear is also very important!

TAKING CARE OF BUSINESS

Extreme athletes choose their equipment carefully, but even the best equipment is useless if it's not in good condition. Athletes check their gear constantly to make sure that there are no loose screws or bolts, cracked plastic, warped wood, or frayed sections of rope. Faulty equipment puts athletes in danger, and it also ruins their ability to perform well. Checking gear doesn't take long, but it may help win a competition or even save a life!

ARMED WITH KNOWLEDGE

Even athletes in full safety gear, such as the BMX rider shown right, can be at risk if they don't know what they're getting themselves into. Athletes depend on knowledge and ability to get themselves out of tough situations safely. Freestylers learn how to **bail**, or escape from a trick that has gone wrong. Before trying new hot spots, athletes talk to local experts about hidden dangers such as rocks under the water's surface or unsafe patches on mountainsides. People who love extreme sports know that quick thinking is their best skill, so they go into new situations prepared with as much knowledge as they can gather.

LEARN MORE

Watching extreme athletes perform can be inspiring. Think you'd like to give it a shot? Fortunately, the extreme popularity of extreme sports makes it easy. There are skilled instructors, helpful equipment shops, and safe places to practice in cities and towns across North America. Many extreme sports are not for everyone, but a few can be tried by just about anyone!

GETTING HELP

The safest and most effective way to learn most sports is with the help of a coach or an experienced athlete. Other athletes at clubs, gyms, or skateparks can also give you tips. Always use proper safety gear when you practice and always have an adult nearby in case you need a hand. Remember, it takes a while to learn the basics and even longer to learn the amazing moves you've seen in this book. Be patient and take your time—your hard work will pay off.

THE LOWDOWN

There are many places to learn about your favorite extreme sports, whether you want to try them or not. Books, magazines, and websites have loads of great information. The web may also connect you with experts who can answer your questions. So, hop online and visit these extreme sites or try a web search for your favorite event.

http://expn.go.com/expn/index
EXPN's website is the ultimate extreme sports source, with up-to-date information about the pros, the X Games, and new sports on the scene.

http://calextremesports.com/xgames-xperience/
This site covers the extreme sports scene in California, providing information on different sports.

GLOSSARY

Note: Boldfaced words that are defined in the text may not appear in the glossary.

artificial Describing a material that is made by people or machines

BMX biking A style of bicycle racing and stunt riding

flip A trick done by turning head over heels while in midair

grab A trick done by grabbing part of the equipment while in midair

grind A trick done by scraping equipment along an obstacle

Gravity Games A series of extreme sports events held annually

halfpipe A U-shaped ramp used for performing freestyle tricks

professional A person who makes their living as an athlete

slalom A type of race in which athletes must move between obstacles on a downhill course

street Describing freestyle extreme sports done on streetside obstacles such as stairs

team A group of professional athletes who travel together but may perform individually

vertical Describing freestyle extreme sports in which athletes use ramps to launch themselves straight into the air

X Games A series of extreme sports events held twice annually

waterskiing A sport in which athletes on skis are pulled by a boat across the surface of a body of water

INDEX